Publisher's Cataloging-In-Publication Data
(Prepared by The Donohue Group, Inc.)

Names: Chapman, Bella, author.
Title: How to have a conflict / by: Bella Chapman.
Description: [Mahomet, Illinois] : [Bella Chapman], [2021] | Title from cover. | Interest age level: 005-008. | Summary: "... follows Kim and her friend Jaime as they navigate a realistic but emotionally complex conflict. The How To Bee watches their interactions unfold and provides helpful tips and comments to the reader. The characters model behavior that empowers kids to set boundaries, engage in healthy discussion, and build rewarding relationships"--Provided by publisher.
Identifiers: ISBN 9781954515000 (hardback) | ISBN 9781954515031 (ePub) | ISBN 9781954515017 (paperback)
Subjects: LCSH: Conflict management--Juvenile fiction. | Interpersonal communication--Juvenile fiction. | Bees--Juvenile fiction. | CYAC: Conflict management--Fiction. | Interpersonal communication--Fiction. | Bees--Fiction.
Classification: LCC PZ7.1.C483 Ho 2021 (print) | LCC PZ7.1.C483 (ebook) | DDC [E]--dc23

Kim was celebrating a special day and was on her way to school with her favorite food for lunch.

She waited patiently through her classes. Finally the bell rang. It was time for lunch.

On the way to her table, she met her friend Jaime.

Kim and Jaime ate together at the same table. Kim was worried because sometimes he ate her food. Usually she just pretended she was okay with that.

Kim opened her lunch and saw all of the delicious foods she had waited so long to eat. Just like she expected, Jaime politely asked if he could have some.

Kim watched him eating her food and became more and more upset. She suddenly started to yell.

Kim started to cry and said "You didn't even wave to me on the bus this morning!"

"Kim needs to stay focused on what is making her upset. Jaime could be confused!"

"This is your fault and you need to fix this!" yelled Kim. She stormed away.

"If Kim offered some ideas to fix the problem, that might help them come up with a good solution together."

"It looks like both friends are upset now..."

LET'S TRY THIS AGAIN

"Jaime, can I talk to you about something?"

"Sure," said Jaime.

"I don't like when you take my food because it makes me feel like I have to give you some, even if I don't want to."

"Asking if it's a good time for a conversation is a great way to start! Ki[m] stayed focused on wha[t] was making her upset."

Jaime said, "I asked beforehand! I don't see why it's a big deal, we always share food and you never got mad before!"

"Kim is sharing how she is feeling, this helps Jaime understand the problem."

Kim replied, "Well, today I had my favorite food and I didn't really want to share even though I said it was okay. When you took my food I felt disappointed and frustrated."

Kim continued, "I know it must have been confusing for you when I told you it was okay and then got upset. I also know you really wanted to share my food. Let's see if we can find a way to make us both happy."

"Kim did a good job listening and understanding her friend's feelings!"

Jaime said, "I'm sorry I made you feel disappointed and frustrated. Let's find a better way."

"Jaime made Kim feel understood by using the words 'disappointed' and 'frustrated,' just like she did. Jaime also did a good job showing that he wants to work together to fix the problem."

"A compromise is a good way to help both friends get what they want."

Kim said, "Maybe we could compromise!"

"What if I eat my food until I am full, and then if I have leftovers, we can share?"

Jaime replied, "That sounds good. I will try to remember not to take your food again unless you're full.

Kim responded, "I'm sorry for not being honest when you asked if it was okay to share. I will try to be more honest with you next time."

"These friends have worked together to solve the problem and both get what they want!"

"It's always nice to say thank you if someone has helped fix the problem!"

"Good work Kim and Jaime!"

For the adults...

Points to remember:

- Conflict isn't good or bad
- Compromise isn't always the best solution

Additional tips:

- Ask if it's a good time for a conversation
- Have a clear goal for your conversation
- Define your needs clearly to your partner
- Have potential solutions ready
- Describe your emotions and why your partner's behavior affects you
- Listen and communicate that you understand their perspective

Further Discussion

If you're not agreeing with someone and you want to talk it out, what should you do or say first?

- Ask if it's a good time for a conversation, find a good environment, have a goal, and define your needs

What might be a good way to show your friend that you care about and understand their opinion, even if you don't agree?

- Repeat back to them the same feeling words they used, let them know you care about them, listen, ask questions if you're confused, and tell them you understand what they're saying

What solutions did Kim offer? Can you think of any different solutions?

- Kim offered the idea to eat her own food until she was full and then give the left overs to Jaime

Can you think of a conflict that you've had? What feelings did you have?

www.ingramcontent.com/pod-product-compliance
Lightning Source LLC
Chambersburg PA
CBHW042316280426
43673CB00080B/383